THE
GOSPELS

adveniat regnum tuum

The Liberal Catholic Rite

PREFACE

This book includes all of the prescribed Gospels from the Third edition of *The Liturgy of the Liberal Catholic Rite*. In addition, a Gospel is included for use at a Holy Eucharist celebrated on the occasion of a Harvest Festival. The Third Edition omitted such a Thanksgiving reading (as well as an Epistle and Collect for the day) but some parishes have found that they use the service. A suggested Gospel will be found in this book on page 80.

This book is printed with 14 point type, making it easier to read in a Sanctuary setting.

Transfiguration, 2007 ✠ The Most Rev. Dean Bekken
Editor

THE GOSPELS

TO BE USED THROUGHOUT THE YEAR

Advent Sunday

The holy Gospel is taken from the twenty-first chapter of the Gospel according to St. Luke, beginning at the twenty-seventh verse.

THEN shall they see the Son of Man coming in a cloud with power and great glory. When these things begin to come to pass, then look up and lift up your heads, for your redemption draweth nigh. And take heed to yourselves, lest at any time your hearts be overcharged with surfeiting, and with the cares of this life, and so that day come upon you unawares. Watch ye therefore, that ye may be accounted worthy to escape all these things that shall come to pass, and to stand before the Son of Man. In your patience possess ye your souls; heaven and earth shall pass away, but My words shall not pass away.

The Second Sunday in Advent

The holy Gospel is taken from the fourth chapter of the Gospel according to St. Mark, beginning at the twenty-fourth verse.

TAKE heed what ye hear; with what measure ye mete, it shall be measured to you; and unto you that hear shall more be given. For he that hath, to him shall be given; and he that hath not, from him shall be taken even that which he hath. So is the kingdom of God, as if a man should cast seed into the ground and should sleep and rise night and day and the seed should spring and grow up, he knoweth not how. For the earth bringeth forth fruit of herself: first the blade, then the ear, and after that the full corn in the ear. But when the fruit is brought forth, immediately he putteth in the sickle, because the harvest is come. Whereunto shall we liken the kingdom of God? Or with what comparison shall we compare it? It is like a grain of mustard seed, which when it is sown in the earth is less than all the seeds that be in the earth; but when it is sown it groweth up, and becometh greater than all herbs, and shooteth out great branches; so that the fowls of the air may lodge under the shadow of it.

The Third Sunday in Advent

The holy Gospel is taken from the first chapter of the Gospel according to St. Mark, beginning at the first verse.

THE beginning of the Gospel of Jesus Christ the Son of God; as it is written in the prophets: Behold, I send my messenger before Thy face, who shall prepare Thy way before Thee; the voice of one crying in the wilderness: Prepare ye the way of the Lord, make His paths straight. John did baptize in the wilderness, and preach the baptism of repentance for the remission of sins. And there went out unto him all the land of Judæa, and they of Jerusalem, and were all baptized of him in the river Jordan, confessing their sins. And John was clothed with camel's hair, and with a girdle of a skin about his loins; and he did eat locusts and wild honey; and preached, saying: There cometh after me One mightier than I, the latchet of whose shoes I am not worthy to stoop down and unloose. I indeed have baptized you with water, but He shall baptize you with the Holy Ghost.

The Fourth Sunday in Advent

The holy Gospel is taken from the thirteenth chapter of the Gospel according to St. John, beginning at the third verse.

JESUS, knowing that the Father had given all things into His hands, and that He was come from God, and went to God, riseth from supper, and laid aside His garments; and took a towel, and girded Himself. After that He poured water into a basin, and began to wash the disciples' feet, and to wipe them with the towel wherewith He was girded. So after He had washed their feet, and had taken His garments, and was set down again, He said unto them: Know ye what I have done to you? Ye call Me Master and Lord; and ye say well, for so I am. If I then, your Lord and Master, have washed your feet, ye also ought to wash one another's feet. For I have given you an example, that ye should do as I have done to you. Amen, Amen, I say unto you: The servant is not greater than his lord; neither he that is sent greater than he that sent him, If ye know these things, happy are ye if ye do them. Amen, Amen, I say unto you: He that receiveth whomsoever I send receiveth Me; and he that receiveth Me receiveth Him that sent Me. A new commandment I give unto you, that ye love one another; as I have loved you, that ye also love one another. By this shall all men know that ye are My disciples, if ye have love one to another.

The Nativity of our Lord, or Christmas Day

The holy Gospel is taken from the first chapter of the Gospel according to St. John, beginning at the first verse.

IN the beginning was the Word, and the Word was with God, and the Word was God. The same was in the beginning with God. All things were made by Him; and without Him was not any thing made that was made. In Him was life, and the life was the light of men. And the light shineth in darkness, and the darkness comprehended it not. There was a man sent from God, whose name was John. The same came for a witness, to bear witness of the light, that all men through him might believe. He was not that light, but was sent to bear witness of that light. That was the true light, which lighteth every man, coming into the world. He was in the world, and the world was made by Him, and the world knew Him not. He came unto His own, and His own received Him not. But as many as received Him, to them gave He power to become the sons of God, even to them that believe on His Name: which were born, not of blood, nor of the will of the flesh, nor of the will of man, but of God. And the Word was made flesh, and dwelt among us (and we beheld His glory, the glory as of the only-begotten of the Father) full of grace and truth.

or

The holy Gospel is taken from the second chapter of the Gospel according to St. Luke, beginning at the first verse.

IT came to pass in those days that there went out a decree from Cæsar Augustus that all the world should be enrolled. And all went to be enrolled, everyone into his own city. And Joseph also went up from Galilee, out of the city of Nazareth, into Judæa, unto the city of David, which is called Bethlehem (because he was of the house and lineage of David) to be enrolled with Mary his espoused wife, being great with child. And so it was that, while they were there, the days were accomplished that she should be delivered. And she brought forth her first-born son, and wrapped Him in swaddling clothes, and laid Him in a manger because there was no room for them in the inn. And there were in the same country shepherds abiding in the field, keeping watch over their flock by night. And, lo, the Angel of the Lord came upon them, and the glory of the Lord shone round about them, and they were sore afraid. And the Angel said unto them: Fear not, for behold, I bring you good tidings of great joy, which shall be to all people. For unto you is born this day in the city of David a Saviour, who is Christ the Lord. And this shall be a sign unto you; ye shall find the babe wrapped in swaddling clothes, lying in a manger. And suddenly there was with the Angel a multitude of the heavenly host praising God, and saying: Glory to God in the highest, and on earth peace, good-will toward men.

The same Gospel shall serve for every day after until New Year's Day, unless otherwise ordered.

New Year's Day

The holy Gospel is taken from the fifth chapter of the Gospel according to St. Matthew, beginning at the fourteenth verse.

YE are the light of the world. Let your light so shine before men, that they may see your good works and glorify your Father who is in heaven. But take heed that ye do not your alms before men, to be seen of them; otherwise ye have no reward of your Father who is in heaven. Therefore when thou doest thine alms, do not sound a trumpet before thee, as the hypocrites do in the synagogues and in the streets, that they may have glory of men. Amen, I say unto you, they have their reward. But when thou doest alms, let not thy left hand know what thy right hand doeth, that thine alms may be in secret; and thy Father who seeth in secret Himself shall reward thee openly. Lay not up for yourselves treasures upon earth, where moth and rust doth corrupt, and where thieves break through and steal; but lay up for yourselves treasures in heaven, where neither moth nor rust doth corrupt, and where thieves do not break through and steal; for where your treasure is, there will your heart be also. The light of the body is the eye; if therefore thine eye be single, thy whole body shall be full of light. Be ye therefore perfect, even as your Father who is in heaven is perfect.

The same Gospel shall serve for every day after, until the Epiphany.

The Epiphany

The holy Gospel is taken from the second chapter of the Gospel according to St. Matthew, beginning at the first verse.

WHEN Jesus was born in Bethlehem of Judæa, in the days of Herod the king, behold, there came wise men from the east to Jerusalem, saying: Where is He that is born King of the Jews? For we have seen His star in the east, and are come to worship Him. When Herod the king heard these things, he was troubled, and all Jerusalem with him; and when he had gathered all the chief priests and scribes of the people together, he demanded of them where Christ should be born. And they said unto him: In Bethlehem of Judæa; for thus it is written by the prophet: And thou, Bethlehem, in the land of Juda, art not the least among the princes of Juda; for out of thee shall come a governor, that shall rule My people Israel. Then Herod, when he had privily called the wise men, inquired of them diligently what time the star appeared. And he sent them to Bethlehem, and said: Go and search diligently for the young Child; and when ye have found Him, bring me word again, that I may come and worship Him also. When they had heard the king, they departed; and lo, the star which they had seen in the east went before them, till it came and stood over where the young Child was. And when they saw the star they rejoiced with exceeding great joy. And when they were come into the house they saw the young Child with Mary His mother, and fell down, and worshipped Him; and when they had opened their treasures, they presented unto Him

gifts, gold and frankincense and myrrh. And being warned of God in a dream that they should not return to Herod, they departed into their own country another way.

The same Gospel shall serve until the Second Sunday after the Epiphany.

The Second Sunday after the Epiphany

The holy Gospel is taken from the seventh chapter of the Gospel according to St. Luke, beginning at the second verse.

NOW a certain centurion's servant, who was very dear unto him, was sick and ready to die. And when he heard of Jesus, he sent unto Him the elders of the Jews, beseeching Him that He would come and heal his servant. And when they came to Jesus, they besought Him instantly, saying that he was worthy for whom He should do this: for he loveth our nation, and he hath built us a synagogue. Then Jesus went with them. And when He was now not far from the house, the centurion sent friends to Him, saying unto Him: Lord, trouble not Thyself; for I am not worthy that Thou shouldest enter under my roof (wherefore neither thought I myself worthy to come unto Thee); but say in a Word, and my servant shall be healed. For I also am a man set under authority, having under me soldiers, and I say unto one: Go, and he goeth; and to another, Come, and he cometh; and to my servant, Do this, and he doeth it. When Jesus heard these things, He marvelled at him, and turned Him about, and said unto the people that followed Him: I say unto you, I have not found so great faith; no, not in Israel. And they that were sent, returning to the house, found the servant whole that had been sick.

𝕮𝖍𝖊 𝕮𝖍𝖎𝖗𝖉 𝕾𝖚𝖓𝖉𝖆𝖞 𝖆𝖋𝖙𝖊𝖗 𝖙𝖍𝖊 𝕰𝖕𝖎𝖕𝖍𝖆𝖓𝖞

The holy Gospel is taken from the twenty-third chapter of the Gospel according to St. Matthew, beginning at the twenty-third verse.

WOE unto you, Scribes and Pharisees, hypocrites! for ye pay tithe of mint and anise and cummin, and have omitted the weightier matters of the law, judgement, mercy and faith; these ought ye to have done, and not to leave the other undone. Ye blind guides, which strain at a gnat and swallow a camel, ye make clean the outside of the cup and of the platter, but within they are full of extortion and excess. Cleanse first that which is within the cup and platter, that the outside of them may be clean also. Ye are like unto whited sepulchres, which indeed appear beautiful outwardly, but within are full of dead men's bones and of all uncleanness. Even so ye outwardly appear righteous unto men, but within ye are full of hypocrisy and iniquity. And He said unto His disciples: Do not ye after their works; for they say and do not. All their works they do for to be seen of men; but whosoever shall exalt himself shall be abased, and he that humbleth himself shall be exalted.

The Fourth Sunday after the Epiphany

The holy Gospel is taken from the sixteenth chapter of the Gospel according to St. John, beginning at the twentieth verse.

AND Jesus said: Ye shall be sorrowful, but your sorrow shall be turned into joy. A little while, and ye shall not see Me; and again a little while, and ye shall see Me. Ye now therefore have sorrow; but I will see you again, and your hearts shall rejoice, and your joy no man taketh from you. Hitherto have ye asked nothing in My Name; ask and ye shall receive, that your joy may be full. This is My commandment, that ye love one another, as I have loved you. Greater love hath no man than this, that a man lay down his life for his friends. Ye are My friends, if ye do whatsoever I command you. Henceforth I call you not servants, for the servant knoweth not what his lord doeth; but I have called you friends, for all things that I have heard of My Father I have made known unto you. These things I have spoken unto you, that My joy might remain in you, and that your joy might be full.

The Fifth Sunday after the Epiphany

The holy Gospel is taken from the twenty-fifth chapter of the Gospel according to St. Matthew, beginning at the fourteenth verse.

THE kingdom of heaven is as a man* travelling into a far country, who called his servants, and delivered unto them his goods. And unto one he gave five talents, to another two, and to another one; to every man according to his several ability; and straightway took his journey. Then he that had received the five talents went and traded with the same, and made them other five talents. And likewise he that had received two, he also gained other two. But he that had received one went and digged in the earth, and hid his lord's money. After a long time the lord of those servants cometh, and reckoneth with them. And so he that had received five talents came and brought other five talents, saying: Lord, thou deliveredst unto me five talents; behold, I have gained beside them five talents more. His lord said unto him: Well done, thou good and faithful servant; thou hast been faithful over a few things, I will make thee ruler over many things; enter thou into the joy of thy lord. He also that had received two talents came and said: Lord, thou deliveredst unto me two talents; behold, I have gained two other talents beside them. His lord said unto him: Well done, good and faithful servant; thou hast been faithful over a few things, I will make thee ruler over many things; enter

---

* The original Greek says, merely, "It is as a man...."

thou into the joy of thy lord. Then he who had received one talent came and said: Lord, I knew thee that thou art an hard man, and I was afraid, and went and hid thy talent in the earth; lo, there thou hast that is thine. But his lord answered and said unto him: Thou wicked and slothful servant, thou oughtest to have put my money to the exchangers, and then at my coming I should have received mine own with usury. Take therefore the talent from him and give it unto him which hath ten talents. For unto every one that hath shall be given, and he shall have abundance; but from him that hath not shall be taken away even that which he hath.

The Sixth Sunday after the Epiphany

The holy Gospel is taken from the twenty-fourth chapter of the Gospel according to St. Matthew, beginning at the thirty-seventh verse.

AS the days of Noah were, so shall the coming of the Son of Man be; for as in the days before the flood they were eating and drinking, marrying and giving in marriage, until the day that Noah entered into the ark, and knew not until the flood came and took them all away; so shall also the Son of Man be. But of that day and that hour knoweth no man; no, not the Angels of heaven, but My Father only. Take heed, watch and pray, lest ye enter into temptation, for ye know not when the time is. The Son of Man is as a man taking a far journey, who left his house, and commanded the porter to watch. Watch ye therefore, lest coming suddenly He find you sleeping. What I say unto you, I say unto all: Watch.

The Sunday called Sexagesima, or the Second Sunday before Lent

The holy Gospel is taken from the twelfth chapter of the Gospel according to St. Mark, beginning at the twenty-eighth verse.

ONE of the scribes came and asked Jesus: Which is the first commandment of all? And Jesus answered him: the first of all the commandments is: Hear, O Israel; the Lord our God is one Lord; and thou shalt love the Lord thy God with all thy heart, and with all thy soul, and with all thy mind, and with all thy strength; this is the first commandment and the second is like unto it, namely, this: Thou shalt love thy neighbour as thyself. There is none other commandment greater than these. And the scribe said unto Him; Well, Master, Thou hast said the truth; for there is one God, and there is none other but He; and to love Him with all the heart, and with all the understanding, and with all thy soul, and with all the strength, and to love his neighbor as himself, is more than all whole burnt offerings and sacrifices. And when Jesus saw that he answered discreetly, He said unto him: thou art not far from the kingdom of God.

The Sunday called Septuagesima, or the third Sunday before Lent

The holy Gospel is taken from the twenty-fifth chapter of the Gospel according to St. Matthew, beginning at the first verse.

THEN shall the kingdom of heaven be likened unto ten virgins, who took their lamps, and went forth to meet the bridegroom. And five of them were wise and five were foolish. They that were foolish took their lamps, and took no oil with them; but the wise took oil in their vessels with their lamps. While the bridegroom tarried, they all slumbered and slept. And at midnight there was a cry made: Behold, the bridegroom cometh; go ye out to meet him. Then all those virgins arose, and trimmed their lamps. And the foolish said unto the wise: Give us of your oil, for our lamps have gone out. But the wise answered saying: Not so, lest there be not enough for us and you; but go ye rather to them that sell, and buy for yourselves. And while they went to buy, the bridegroom came; and they that were ready went in with him to the marriage; and the door was shut. Afterwards came also the other virgins, saying: Lord, Lord, open to us. But he answered and said: Amen, I say unto to you, I know you not. Watch therefore, for ye know neither the day nor the hour wherein the Son of Man cometh.

The Sunday called Quinquagesima, or the Sunday before Lent

The holy Gospel is taken from the twentieth chapter of the Gospel according to St. Matthew, beginning at the first verse.

THE kingdom of heaven is like unto a man that is an householder, who went out early in the morning to hire labourers into his vineyard. And when he had agreed with the labourers for a penny a day, he sent them into his vineyard. And he went out about the third hour, and saw others standing idle in the marketplace, and said unto them: Go ye also into the vineyard, and whatsoever is right I will give you. And they went their way. Again he went out about the sixth and ninth hour, and did likewise. And about the eleventh hour he went out, and found others standing idle, and saith unto them: Why stand ye here all the day idle? They say unto him: Because no man hath hired us. He saith unto them: Go ye also into the vineyard; and whatsoever is right, that shall ye receive. So when even was come, the lord of the vineyard saith unto his steward: Call the labourers, and give them their hire, beginning from the last unto the first. And when they came that were hired about the eleventh hour, they received every man a penny. But when the first came, they supposed that they should have received more; and they likewise received every man a penny. And when they had received it, they murmured against the goodman of the house, saying: These last have wrought but one hour, and thou hast made them equal unto us, who have borne the burden and heat of the day. But he answered one of them, and said: Friend, I do thee no wrong; didst not thou agree With me for a penny? Take that thine is, and go thy way; I will give unto this last even as unto thee. Is it not lawful for me to do what I will with mine own? Is thine eye evil, because I am good? So the last shall be first, and the first last; for many be called, but few chosen.

This Gospel shall serve until the First Day of Lent.

The First Day of Lent, anciently called Ash-Wednesday

The holy Gospel is taken from the third chapter of the Gospel according to St. John, beginning at the third verse.

JESUS said unto Nicodemus: Amen, I say unto thee, except a man be born again, he cannot see the kingdom of God. Nicodemus saith unto Him: How can a man be born when he is old? And Jesus answered: Amen, Amen, I say unto thee, except a man be born of water and of the Spirit, he cannot enter into the kingdom of God. That which is born of the flesh is flesh, and that which is born of the Spirit is spirit. Marvel not that I said unto thee, ye must be born again. The wind bloweth where it listeth, and thou hearest the sound thereof, but canst not tell whence it cometh and whither it goeth; so is everyone that is born of the Spirit. Nicodemus said: How can these things be? Jesus answered: Amen, Amen, I say unto thee, we speak that we do know, and testify that we have seen; and ye receive not our witness. If I have told you earthly things, and ye believe not, how shall ye believe, if I tell you of heavenly things? And no man hath ascended up to heaven but He that came down from heaven, even the Son of Man who is in heaven. And as Moses lifted up the serpent in the wilderness, even so must the Son of Man be lifted up: that whosoever believeth may in Him have eternal life.

The same Gospel shall serve for every day after until the next Sunday.

The First Sunday in Lent

The holy Gospel is taken from the third chapter of the Gospel according to St. John, beginning at the sixteenth verse.

GOD so loved the world that He gave His only-begotten Son, that whosoever believeth in Him should not perish, but have everlasting life. For God sent not His Son into the world to condemn the world, but that the world through Him might be saved. He that believeth on Him is not condemned; but he that believeth not is condemned already, because he hath not believed in the Name of the only-begotten Son of God. And this is the condemnation, that light is come into the world, and men loved darkness rather than light, because their deeds were evil. For everyone that doeth evil hateth the light, neither cometh to the light, lest his deeds should be reproved. But he that doeth truth cometh to the light, that his deeds may be made manifest, that they are wrought in God.

The Second Sunday in Lent

The holy Gospel is taken from the sixth chapter of the Gospel according to St. Luke, beginning at the forty-first verse.

WHY beholdest thou the mote that is in thy brother's eye, but perceivest not the beam that is in thine own eye? How canst thou say to thy brother: Brother, let me pull out the mote that is in thine eye; when thou thyself beholdest not the beam that is in thine own eye? Thou hypocrite, cast out first the beam out of thine own eye, and then shalt thou see clearly to pull out the mote that is in thy brother's eye. For a good tree bringeth not forth corrupt fruit; neither doth a corrupt tree bring forth good fruit. For every tree is known by his own fruit; for of thorns men do not gather figs, nor of a bramble-bush gather they grapes. A good man out of the good treasure of his heart bringeth forth that which is good; and an evil man out of the evil treasure of his heart bringeth forth that which is evil; for of the abundance of the heart his mouth speaketh.

The Third Sunday in Lent

The holy Gospel is taken from the eighth chapter of the Gospel according to St. John, beginning at the third verse.

THE Pharisees brought unto Jesus a woman taken in adultery, and when they had set her in the midst, they said unto Him: Master, this woman was taken in adultery, in the very act; now Moses in the Law commanded us that such should be stoned; but what sayest Thou? This they said, tempting Him, that they might have wherewith to accuse Him. But Jesus stooped down, and with His finger wrote on the ground, as though He heard them not. So when they continued asking Him, He lifted Himself up, and said unto them: He that is without sin among you, let him first cast a stone at her. And again He stooped down and wrote on the ground. And they who heard it, being convicted by their own conscience, went out one by one, beginning at the eldest, even unto the last; and Jesus was left alone, and the woman standing in the midst. When Jesus had lifted up Himself, and saw none but the woman, He said unto her: Woman, where are those thine accusers? Hath no man condemned thee? She said: No man, Lord. And Jesus said unto her: Neither do I condemn thee; go, and sin no more.

The Fourth Sunday in Lent, or Refreshment Sunday

The holy Gospel is taken from the sixth chapter of the Gospel according to St. John, beginning at the third verse.

JESUS went up into a mountain, and there He sat with His disciples. And when He lifted up His eyes, and saw a great company come unto Him, He saith unto Philip: Whence shall we buy bread, that these may eat? Philip answered: Two hundred pennyworth of bread is not sufficient for them, that every one of them may take a little. One of His disciples, Andrew, Simon Peter's brother, saith unto Him: There is a lad here, who hath five barley loaves, and two small fishes; but what are they among so many? Jesus said: Make the men sit down. Now there was much grass in the place. So the men sat down, in number about five thousand. And Jesus took the loaves; and when He had given thanks, He distributed to the disciples, and the disciples to them that were set down; and likewise of the fishes as much as they would. When they were filled, he said unto His disciples: Gather up the fragments that remain, that nothing be lost. Therefore they gathered them together, and filled twelve baskets with the fragments of the five barley loaves which remained over and above unto them that had eaten. Then those men, when they had seen this miracle which Jesus did, said: This is of a truth that prophet which should come into the world.

The Fifth Sunday in Lent, or Passion Sunday

The holy Gospel is taken from the eighteenth chapter of the Gospel according to St. Luke, beginning at the ninth verse.

HE spake this parable unto certain who trusted in themselves that they were righteous, and despised others: Two men went up into the temple to pray; the one a Pharisee, and the other a publican. The Pharisee stood and prayed thus with himself: God, I thank Thee that I am not as other men are, extortioners, unjust, or even as this publican. I fast twice in the week, I give tithes of all that I possess. And the publican, standing afar off, would not lift up so much as his eyes unto heaven, but smote upon his breast, saying: God be merciful to me, a sinner. I tell you, this man went down to his house justified rather than the other; for every one that exalteth himself shall be abased, and he that humbleth himself shall be exalted. And they brought unto Him also infants, that He should touch them; but when His disciples saw it, they rebuked them. But Jesus called them unto Him, and said: Suffer little children to come unto Me, and forbid them not; for of such is the kingdom of God. Amen, I say unto you: Whosoever shall not receive the kingdom of God as a little child shall in no wise enter therein.

The Sunday Next before Easter or Palm Sunday

The holy Gospel is taken from the twenty-first chapter of the Gospel according to St. Matthew, beginning at the first verse.

WHEN they drew nigh unto Jerusalem and were come to Bethphage unto the Mount of Olives, then sent Jesus two disciples, saying unto them: Go unto the village over against you, and straightway ye shall find an ass tied and a colt with her; loose them and bring them unto Me. And if any man say aught unto you, ye shall say: The Lord hath need of them; and straightway he will send them. And the disciples went and did as Jesus commanded them, and brought the ass and the colt, and put on them their clothes, and they set Him thereon. And a very great multitude spread their garments in the way; others cut down branches from the trees and strewed them in the way. And the multitude that went before and that followed cried saying: Hosanna to the Son of David; Blessed is He that cometh in the Name of the Lord; Hosanna in the highest. And when He was come into Jerusalem all the city was moved saying: Who is this? And the multitude said: This is Jesus the prophet of Nazareth in Galilee.

The same Gospel shall serve for every day until Maundy Thursday.

Maundy Thursday

The holy Gospel is taken from the sixth chapter of the Gospel according to St. John, beginning at the forty-seventh verse.

AMEN, Amen, I say unto you, he that believeth on Me hath everlasting life. I am that Bread of life. This is the Bread which cometh down from heaven, that a man may eat thereof, and not die. I am the living Bread which came down from heaven; if any man eat of this Bread, he shall live for ever; and the Bread that I will give is My Flesh, which I will give for the life of the world. The Jews therefore strove among themselves, saying: How can this man give us his flesh to eat? Then Jesus said unto them: Amen, Amen, I say unto you, except ye eat the Flesh of the Son of Man, and drink His Blood, ye have no life in you; whoso eateth My Flesh and drinketh My Blood, hath eternal life; and I will raise him up at the last day. For My Flesh is meat indeed, and My Blood is drink indeed. He that eateth My Flesh, and drinketh My Blood, dwelleth in Me, and I in him. As the living Father hath sent Me, and I live by the Father; so he that eateth Me even he shall live by Me. This is that Bread which came down from heaven; not as your fathers did eat manna, and are dead; he that eateth of this Bread shall live for ever.

Easter Day

The holy Gospel is taken from the twenty-eighth chapter of the Gospel according to St. Matthew, beginning at the first verse.

AS it began to dawn towards the first day of the week came Mary Magdalene and the other Mary to see the sepulchre. And, behold, there was a great earthquake, for the Angel of the Lord descended from heaven, and came and rolled back the stone from the door and sat upon it. His countenance was like lightning, and his raiment white as snow, and for fear of him the keepers did shake, and became as dead men. And the Angel said unto the women: Fear not ye, for I know that ye seek Jesus, who was crucified. Why seek ye the living amidst the dead? He is not here; He has risen, as He said. Come, see the place where the Lord lay. And go quickly and tell His disciples that He is risen from the dead. And they departed quickly from the sepulchre with fear and great joy, and did run to bring His disciples word. And as they went to tell His disciples, behold, Jesus met them, saying: All hail. And they came and took Him by the feet, and worshipped Him.

The First Sunday after Easter, or Low Sunday

The holy Gospel is taken from the twenty-fourth chapter of the Gospel according to St. Luke, beginning at the thirteenth verse.

BEHOLD, two of His disciples went that same day to a village called Emmaus, which was from Jerusalem about three-score furlongs. And they talked together of all these things which had happened. And it came to pass that, while they communed together and reasoned, Jesus Himself drew near, and went with them. But their eyes were holden, that they should not know Him. And He said unto them: What manner of communications are these that ye have one to another, as ye walk, and are sad? And the one of them, whose name was Cleopas, answering, said unto Him: Art thou only a stranger in Jerusalem, and hast not known the things which are come to pass there in these days? And He said unto them: What things? And they said unto Him: Concerning Jesus of Nazareth, who was a prophet mighty in deed and word, before God and all the people; and how the chief priests and our rulers delivered Him to be condemned to death, and have crucified Him. But we trusted that it had been He who should have redeemed Israel; and, beside all this, to-day is the third day since these things were done. Yea, and certain women also of our company made us astonished, who were early at the sepulchre; and when they found not His body, they came, saying that they had also seen a vision of Angels, which said that He was alive. And certain of them who were with us went to the sepulchre, and found it even so as the women had said; but Him they saw not. Then He said unto them: O fools and slow of heart to believe all that the prophets have spoken; ought not Christ to have suffered these things, and to enter into His glory? And, beginning at Moses, and all the prophets, He expounded unto them in all the Scriptures the things concerning Himself. And they drew nigh unto the village wither they went, and He made as though He would have gone further; but they constrained Him, saying: Abide with us, for it is towards evening, and the day is far spent. And He went in to tarry with them. And it came to pass, as He sat at meat with them, He took bread, and blessed it, and brake, and gave to them. And their eyes were opened, and they knew Him, and He vanished out of their sight. And they said one to another: Did not our heart burn within us while He talked with us by the way, and while He opened to us the Scriptures? And they rose up the same hour and returned to Jerusalem, and found the eleven gathered together, and them that were with them, saying: The Lord is risen indeed and hath appeared to Simon. And they told what things were done in the way, and how He was known of them in breaking of bread.

The Second Sunday after Easter

The holy Gospel is taken from the twentieth chapter of the Gospel according to St. John, beginning at the nineteenth verse.

THE same day at evening, being the first day of the week, when the doors were shut where the disciples were assembled for fear of the Jews, came Jesus and stood in the midst, and saith unto them: Peace be unto you. And when He had so said, He showed unto them His hands and His side. Then were the disciples glad when they saw the Lord. Then said Jesus to them again: Peace be unto you; as My Father hath sent Me, even so send I you. And when He had said this, He breathed on them, and saith unto them: Receive ye the Holy Ghost. Whosoever sins ye remit, they are remitted unto them; and whosoever sins ye retain, they are retained.

The Third Sunday after Easter

The holy Gospel is taken from the twenty-fourth chapter of the Gospel according to St. Luke, beginning at the thirty-sixth verse.

JESUS Himself stood in the midst of them, and saith unto them: Peace be unto you. And He said: These are the words which I spake unto you while I was yet with you, that all things must be fulfilled which were written in the law of Moses and in the Prophets and in the Psalms concerning Me. Then opened He their understanding, that they might understand the Scriptures, and said unto them: Thus it is written, and thus it behoved Christ to suffer, and to rise from the dead the third day; and that repentance and remission of sins should be preached in His Name among all nations, beginning at Jerusalem. And ye are witnesses of these things.

The Fourth Sunday after Easter

The holy Gospel is taken from the sixteenth chapter of the Gospel according to St. Mark, beginning at the first verse.

WHEN the sabbath was past, Mary Magdalene, and Mary the mother of James, and Salome, had bought sweet spices, that they might come and anoint Him. And very early in the morning the first day of the week, they came unto the sepulchre at the rising of the sun. And they said among themselves: Who shall roll us away the stone from the door of the sepulchre? And when they looked they saw that the stone was rolled away: for it was very great. And, entering into the sepulchre, they saw a young man sitting on the right side, clothed in a long white garment, and they were affrighted. And he saith unto them: Be not affrighted; ye seek Jesus of Nazareth who was crucified. He is risen; He is not here; behold the place where they laid Him. But go your way, tell His disciples and Peter that He goeth before you into Galilee: there shall ye see Him, as He said unto you.

The Fifth Sunday after Easter

The holy Gospel is taken from the sixteenth chapter of the Gospel according to St. Mark, beginning at the ninth verse.

NOW when Jesus was risen early the first day of the week, He appeared first to Mary Magdalene, out of whom He had east seven devils. And she went and told them that had been with Him, as they mourned and wept. And they, when they had heard that He was alive, and had been seen of her, believed not. After that He appeared in another form unto two of them, as they walked, and went into the country. And they went and told it unto the residue, neither believed they them. Afterward He appeared unto the eleven as they sat at meat, and upbraided them with their unbelief and hardness of heart, because they believed not them who had seen Him after He was risen. And He said unto them: Go ye into all the world, and preach the Gospel to every creature.

The Ascension Day

The holy Gospel is taken from the twenty-fourth chapter of the Gospel according to St. Luke, beginning at the forty-ninth verse.

BEHOLD, I send the promise of My Father upon you: but tarry ye in the city of Jerusalem, until ye be endued with power from on high. And He led them out as far as to Bethany, and He lifted up His hands, and blessed them. And it came to pass, while He blessed them, He was parted from them, and carried up into heaven. And they worshipped Him, and returned to Jerusalem with great joy, and were continually in the temple, praising and blessing God. Amen.

The same Gospel shall serve for nine days after.

After the Gospel on Ascension Day, when the Deacon has censed the celebrant, the latter shall reverently extinguish the paschal candle, saying:

The great forty days are over; the Lord hath ascended into heaven; and so in His Name I extinguish this paschal candle, which for forty days has symbolized among us His risen body, for a token that as its light, leaving this lower world, passes to higher realms, so may we in heart and mind thither ascend and with Him continually dwell.

Whitsunday

The holy Gospel is taken from the fourteenth chapter of the Gospel according to St. John, beginning at the sixteenth verse.

JESUS said unto His disciples: I will pray the Father, and He shall give you another Comforter, that He may abide with you for ever; even the Spirit of Truth, whom the world cannot receive, because it seeth Him not, neither knoweth Him; but ye know Him; for He dwelleth with you, and shall be in you. I will not leave you comfortless; I will come to you. Yet a little while, and the world seeth Me no more; but ye see Me; because I live, ye shall live also. The Comforter, who is the Holy Ghost, whom the Father will send in My Name, He shall teach you all things, and bring all things to your remembrance, whatsoever I have said unto you. Peace I leave with you, My peace I give unto you: not as the world giveth, give I unto you. Let not your heart be troubled, neither let it be afraid.

Trinity Sunday

The Holy Gospel is taken from the fourteenth chapter of the Gospel according to St. John, beginning at the sixth verse.

JESUS said: I am the Way, the Truth, and the Life; no man cometh unto the Father, but by Me. He that hath seen Me hath seen the Father; for I am in the Father, and the Father in Me. I and my Father are one; as the Father hath loved Me, so I loved you; and this is My Father's commandment, that ye love one another, as I have loved you. When the Comforter is come, whom I send unto you from the Father, even the Spirit of Truth, who proceedeth from the Father, He shall testify of Me. And ye also shall bear witness, because ye have been with Me from the beginning. By this shall all men know that ye are My disciples, if ye have love one to another.

Corpus Christi

The holy Gospel is taken from the sixth chapter of the Gospel according to St. John, beginning at the forty-seventh verse.

AMEN, Amen, I say unto you: He that believeth on Me hath everlasting life. I am that Bread of life. This is the Bread which cometh down from heaven, that a man may eat thereof, and not die. I am the living Bread which came down from heaven; if any man eat of this Bread, he shall live for ever; and the Bread that I will give is My Flesh, which I will give for the life of the world. The Jews therefore strove among themselves, saying: How can this man give us his flesh to eat? Then Jesus said unto them: Amen, Amen, I say unto you: Except ye eat the Flesh of the Son of Man, and drink His Blood, ye have no life in you. Whoso eateth My Flesh, and drinketh My Blood, hath eternal life; and I will raise him up at the last day, For My Flesh is meat indeed, and My Blood is drink indeed. He that eateth My Flesh and drinketh My Blood, dwelleth in Me, and I in him. As the living Father hath sent Me, and I live by the Father; so he that eateth Me, even he shall live by Me. This is that Bread which came down from Heaven; not as your fathers did eat manna, and are dead; he that eateth of this Bread shall live for ever.

The Second Sunday after Trinity

The holy Gospel is taken from the twelfth chapter of the Gospel according to St. John, beginning at the thirty-second verse.

I, if I be lifted up from the earth, will draw all men unto Me. Yet a little while is the light with you. Walk while ye have the light, lest darkness come upon you; for he that walketh in darkness knoweth not whither he goeth. While ye have light, believe in the light, that ye may be the children of light. He that believeth on Me, believeth not on Me only, but on Him that sent Me; and he that seeth Me, seeth Him that sent Me. I am come a light into the world, that whosoever believeth on Me should not abide in darkness.

The Third Sunday after Trinity

The holy Gospel is taken from the first chapter of the Gospel according to St. Luke, beginning at the eighth verse.

WHILE Zacharias executed the priest's office before God in the order of his course, according to the custom of the priest's office, his lot was to burn incense when he went into the temple of the Lord. And the whole multitude of the people were praying without at the time of incense. And there appeared unto him an Angel of the Lord, standing on the right side of the altar of incense. And when Zacharias saw him, he was troubled, and fear fell upon him; but the Angel said unto him: Fear not, Zacharias; thy prayer is heard, and thou shalt have joy and gladness. I am Gabriel, that stand in the Presence of God; and I am sent to speak unto thee, and to show thee these glad tidings.

The Fourth Sunday after Trinity

The holy Gospel is taken from the fifteenth chapter of the Gospel according to St. John, beginning at the first verse.

I AM the true vine, and My Father is the Husbandman. I am the Vine, ye are the branches. Abide in Me, and I in you. As the branch cannot bear fruit of itself, except it abide in the vine; no more can ye, except ye abide in Me. He that abideth in Me, and I in him, the same bringeth forth much fruit; for without Me ye can do nothing. Herein is My Father glorified, that ye bear much fruit; so shall ye be My disciples. As the Father hath loved Me, so have I loved you; continue ye in My love. If ye keep My commandments, ye shall abide in My love; even as I have kept My Father's commandments, and abide in His love. These things have I spoken unto you, that My joy might remain in you, and that your joy might be full. These things I command you, that ye love one another.

The Fifth Sunday after Trinity

The holy Gospel is taken from the fourteenth chapter of the Gospel according to St. John, beginning at the eighteenth verse.

JESUS said: I will not leave you comfortless; I will come to you. Because I live, ye shall live also. At that day ye shall know that I am in My Father, and ye in Me, and I in you. He that hath My commandments and keepeth them, he it is that loveth Me; and he that loveth Me shall be loved of My Father, and I will love him, and will manifest Myself to him. If a man love Me, he will keep My words; and My Father will love him, and We will come unto him, and make Our abode with him. He that keepeth not My sayings loveth Me not. Peace I leave with you, My peace I give unto you; not as the world giveth, give I unto you. Let not your heart be troubled, neither let it be afraid.

The Sixth Sunday after Trinity

The holy Gospel is taken from the twenty-fifth chapter of the Gospel according to St. Matthew, beginning at the thirty-first verse.

WHEN the Son of Man shall come in His glory, and all the holy Angels with Him, then shall He sit upon the throne of His glory. Before Him shall be gathered all nations, and He shall separate them one from another, as a shepherd divideth his sheep from the goats; and He shall set the sheep on His right hand, but the goats on the left. Then shall the King say unto them on His right hand: Come, ye blessed of My Father, inherit the kingdom prepared for you from the foundation of the world. For I was an hungred and ye gave Me meat; I was thirsty and ye gave Me drink; I was a stranger, and ye took Me in; naked, and ye clothed Me; I was sick, and ye visited Me; I was in prison, and ye came unto Me. Then shall the righteous answer Him, saying: Lord, when saw we Thee an hungred, and fed Thee? or thirsty, and gave Thee drink? When saw we Thee a stranger, and took Thee in? or naked, and clothed Thee? Or when saw we Thee sick, or in prison, and came unto Thee? And the King shall answer and say unto them: Amen, I say unto you, inasmuch as ye have done it unto one of the least of these My brethren, ye have done it unto Me. Then shall He say also unto them on the left hand: Depart from Me. For I was an hungred, and ye gave Me no meat; I was thirsty, and ye gave Me no drink; I was a stranger, and ye took Me not in; naked, and ye clothed Me not; sick, and in prison, and ye visited Me not. Then shall they also answer Him saying: Lord, when saw we Thee an hungred, or athirst, or a stranger, or naked, or sick, or in prison, and did not minister unto Thee? Then shall He answer them, saying: Amen, I say unto you, inasmuch as ye did it not to one of the least of these, ye did it not to Me.

𝔗𝔥𝔢 𝔖𝔢𝔳𝔢𝔫𝔱𝔥 𝔖𝔲𝔫𝔡𝔞𝔶 𝔞𝔣𝔱𝔢𝔯 𝔗𝔯𝔦𝔫𝔦𝔱𝔶

The holy Gospel is taken from the seventeenth chapter of the Gospel according to St. John, beginning at the eleventh verse.

AND Jesus said: Holy Father, keep through Thine own Name those whom Thou hast given Me, that they may be one, as We are. I pray not that Thou shouldest take them out of the world, but that Thou shouldest keep them from the evil. They are not of the world, even as I am not of the world. Sanctify them through Thy truth; Thy word is truth. Neither pray I for these alone, but for them also who shall believe on Me through their word; that they all may be one, as Thou, Father, art in Me, and I in Thee, that they also may be one in Us. The glory which Thou gavest Me I have given them; that they may be one, even as We are one. I in them, and Thou in Me, that they may be made perfect in one; and that the world may know that Thou hast loved them, as Thou hast loved Me. Father, I will that they also, whom Thou hast given Me, be with Me where I am. I have declared unto them Thy Name, that the love wherewith Thou hast loved Me may be in them, and I in them.

The Eighth Sunday after Trinity

The holy Gospel is taken from the second chapter of the Gospel according to St. Luke, beginning at the fortieth verse.

THE child Jesus grew, and waxed strong in spirit, filled with wisdom; and the grace of God was upon Him. Now His parents went to Jerusalem every year at the feast of the passover. And when He was twelve years old, they went up to Jerusalem after the custom of the feast. And when they had fulfilled the days, as they returned, the child Jesus tarried behind in Jerusalem; and Joseph and His mother knew not of it. But they, supposing Him to have been in the company, went a day's journey; and they sought Him among their kinsfolk and acquaintance. And when they found Him not, they turned back again to Jerusalem, seeking Him. And it came to pass, that after three days they found Him in the temple, sitting in the midst of the doctors, both hearing them, and asking them questions. And all that heard Him were astonished at His understanding and answers. And when they saw Him they were amazed: and His mother said unto Him: Son, why hast Thou thus dealt with us? Behold, Thy father and I have sought Thee sorrowing. And He said unto them: How is it that ye sought Me? Wist ye not that I must be about My Father's business? And they understood not the saying which He spake unto them. But His mother kept all these sayings in her heart. And Jesus increased in wisdom and stature, and in favour with God and man.

The Ninth Sunday after Trinity

The holy Gospel is taken from the twelfth chapter of the Gospel according to St. John, beginning at the twenty-third verse.

JESUS said: The hour is come that the Son of Man should be glorified. Amen, Amen, I say unto you, except a corn of wheat fall into the ground and die, it abide alone; but if it die, it bringeth forth much fruit. He that loveth his life shall lose it; and he that hateth his life in this world shall keep it unto life eternal. If any man serve Me, let him follow Me; and where I am, there shall also My servant be. Father, glorify Thy Name. Then came there a voice from heaven saying: I have both glorified it, and will glorify it again.

The Tenth Sunday after Trinity

The holy Gospel is taken from the fourth chapter of the Gospel according to St. John, beginning at the nineteenth verse.

THE woman of Samaria saith unto Him: Sir, I perceive that Thou art a prophet. Our fathers worshipped in this mountain; and ye say that in Jerusalem is the place where men ought to worship. Jesus said unto her: Believe Me, the hour cometh when ye shall neither in this mountain, nor yet in Jerusalem, worship the Father. Ye worship ye know not what; we know what we worship. But the hour cometh, and now is, when the true worshippers shall worship the Father in spirit and in truth, for the Father seeketh such to worship Him. God is a Spirit; and they that worship Him must worship Him in spirit and in truth The woman saith unto Him: I know that Messias cometh who is called the Christ; when He is come, He will tell us all things. Jesus said unto her: I that speak unto thee am He.

The Eleventh Sunday after Trinity

The holy Gospel is taken from the twelfth chapter of the Gospel according to St. Luke, beginning at the fifty-fourth verse.

JESUS said unto the people: When ye see a cloud rise out of the west, straightway ye say: There cometh a shower and so it is. And when ye see the south wind ye say: There will he heat; and it cometh to pass. Ye can discern the face of the sky and of the earth; but how is it that ye do not discern this time? Yea, and why even of yourselves judge ye not what is right? Seek not ye what ye shall eat or what ye shall drink, for all these do the nations of the world seek after. Rather seek ye the kingdom of God and His righteousness, and all these things shall be added unto you. Fear not, little flock; for it is your Father's good pleasure to give you the kingdom.

The Twelfth Sunday after Trinity

The holy Gospel is taken from the fifth chapter of the Gospel according to St. Matthew, beginning at the seventeenth verse.

THINK not that I am come to destroy the law or the prophets; I am not come to destroy, but to fulfil. Amen, I say unto you: Till heaven and earth pass, one jot or one tittle shall in no wise pass from the law till all be fulfilled. Whosoever therefore shall break one of these least commandments, and shall teach men so, he shall be called least in the kingdom of heaven; but whosoever shall do and teach them, the same shall be called great in the kingdom of heaven. For I say unto you that except your righteousness shall exceed the righteousness of the scribes and Pharisees, ye shall in no case enter into the kingdom of heaven. Ye have heard that it hath been said: Thou shalt love thy neighbour and hate thine enemy. But I say unto you: Love your enemies; bless them that curse you, do good to them that hate you, and pray for them that despitefully use you and persecute you; that ye may be the children of your Father who is in heaven. For He maketh His sun to rise on the evil and on the good, and sendeth rain on the just and on the unjust.

The Thirteenth Sunday after Trinity

The holy Gospel is taken from the seventh chapter of the Gospel according to St. Matthew, beginning at the sixteenth verse.

YE shall know them by their fruits. Do men gather grapes of thorns, or figs of thistles? Even so, every good tree bringeth forth good fruit; but a corrupt tree bringeth forth evil fruit. A good tree cannot bring forth evil fruit, neither can a corrupt tree bring forth good fruit. Wherefore by their fruits ye shall know them. Not every one that saith unto Me, Lord, Lord, shall enter into the kingdom of heaven; but he that doeth the will of My Father who is in heaven. Many will say to Me: Lord, Lord, have we not prophesied in Thy Name? and in Thy Name have cast out devils? and in Thy Name done many wonderful works? Then will I profess unto them: I never knew you; depart from Me, ye that work iniquity. Therefore whosoever heareth these sayings of Mine and doeth them, I will liken him unto a wise man, who built his house upon a rock; and the rain descended, and the floods came, and the winds blew, and beat upon that house; and it fell not, for it was founded upon a rock. But everyone that heareth these sayings of Mine and doeth them not, shall be likened unto a foolish man who built his house upon the sand; and the rain descended, and the floods came, and the winds blew, and beat upon that house; and it fell; and great was the fall of it.

Fourteenth Sunday after Trinity

The holy Gospel is taken from the ninth chapter of the Gospel according to St. Matthew, beginning at the second verse.

THEY brought to Him a man sick of the palsy, lying on a bed; and Jesus, seeing their faith, said unto the sick of the palsy: Son, be of good cheer; thy sins be forgiven thee. But certain of the scribes said within themselves: This man blasphemeth. And Jesus, knowing their thoughts, said: Wherefore think ye evil in your hearts? For whether is easier, to say, Thy sins be forgiven thee, or to say, Arise and walk? But that ye may know that the Son of Man hath power on earth to forgive sins (then saith He to the sick of the palsy): Arise, take up thy bed, and go unto thine house. And he arose and departed to his house. And when the multitude saw it, they marvelled, and glorified God, who had given such power unto men.

The Fifteenth Sunday after Trinity

The holy Gospel is taken from the tenth chapter of the Gospel according to St. Luke, beginning at the twenty-fifth verse.

A CERTAIN lawyer stood up saying: Master, what shall I do to inherit eternal life? Jesus said unto him: What is written in the law? How readest thou? And he answering said: Thou shalt love the Lord thy God with all thy heart, and with all thy soul, and with all thy strength, and with all thy mind; and thy neighbour as thyself. Jesus said unto him: Thou hast answered right; this do and thou shalt live. But he, willing to justify himself, said unto Jesus: And who is my neighbour? And Jesus answering said: A certain man went down from Jerusalem to Jericho and fell among thieves, who stripped him of his raiment and wounded him, and departed, leaving him half dead. And by chance there came down a certain priest that way; and when he saw him, he passed by on the other side. Likewise a Levite, when he was at the place, came and looked on him, and passed by on the other side. But a certain Samaritan, as he journeyed, came where he was; and when he saw him, he had compassion on him, and went to him and bound up his wounds, pouring in oil and wine, and set him on his own beast, and brought him to an inn, and took care of him. And on the morrow when he departed, he took out two pence and gave them to the host, and said unto him: Take care of him; and whatever thou spendest more, when I come again I will repay thee. Which now of these three, thinkest thou, was neighbour unto him that fell among the thieves? And the lawyer said: He that showed mercy on him. Then said Jesus unto him: Go, and do thou likewise.

The Sixteenth Sunday after Trinity

The holy Gospel is taken from the fifth chapter of the Gospel according to St. John, beginning at the twenty-fifth verse.

AMEN, Amen, I say unto you, the hour is coming, and now is, when the dead shall hear the voice of the Son of God; and they that hear shall live. For as the Father hath life in Himself, so hath He given to the Son to have life in Himself, and hath given Him authority to execute judgement also, because He is the Son of Man. Marvel not at this; for the hour is coming in which all that are in the graves shall hear His voice and shall come forth: they that have done good unto the resurrection of life, and they that have done evil unto the resurrection of condemnation. As I hear, I judge, and My judgement is just; for the Son of Man shall come in the glory of His Father with His Angels, and then shall He reward every man according to his works.

The Seventeenth Sunday after Trinity

The holy Gospel is taken from the eleventh chapter of the Gospel according to St. Matthew, beginning at the seventh verse.

JESUS began to say unto the multitudes concerning John: What went ye out into the wilderness to see? A reed shaken with the wind? But what went ye out for to see? A man clothed in soft raiment? Behold, they that wear soft clothing are in kings' houses. But what went ye out for to see? A prophet? Yea, I say unto you, and more than a prophet. For this is he of whom it is written: Behold, I send My messenger before thy face, who shall prepare thy way before thee. Amen, I say unto you, among them that are born of women there hath not risen a greater than John the Baptist: notwithstanding, he that is least in the kingdom of heaven is greater than he. And from the days of John the Baptist until now the kingdom of heaven suffereth violence, and the violent take it by force. For all the prophets and the law prophesied until John. And if ye will receive it, this is Elias, who was for to come. He that hath ears to hear, let him hear.

The Eighteenth Sunday after Trinity

The holy Gospel is taken from the fourteenth chapter of the Gospel according to St. John, beginning at the first verse.

LET not your heart be troubled; ye believe in God, believe also in Me. In My Father's house are many mansions; if it were not so, I would have told you. I go to prepare a place for you. And if I go and prepare a place for you, I will come again, and receive you unto Myself; that where I am, there ye may be also. And whither I go ye know, and the way ye know. Thomas saith unto Him: Lord, we know not whither Thou goest; and how can we know the way? Jesus saith unto him: I am the way, the truth, and the life; no man cometh unto the Father, but by Me. If ye had known Me, ye should have known My Father also; and from henceforth ye know Him, and have seen Him. Philip saith unto Him: Lord, show us the Father, and it sufficeth us. Jesus said unto him: Have I been so long time with you, and yet hast thou not known Me, Philip? He that hath seen Me hath seen the Father.

The Nineteenth Sunday after Trinity

The holy Gospel is taken from the tenth chapter of the Gospel according to St. John, beginning at the seventh verse.

THEN said Jesus unto them again: Amen, Amen, I say unto you, I am the door of the sheep. By Me if any man enter in, he shall be saved, and shall go in and out, and find pasture. I am come that they might have life, and that they might have it more abundantly. I am the good shepherd; the good shepherd giveth his life for the sheep. The hireling fleeth, because he is an hireling, and careth not for the sheep. I am the good shepherd, and know My sheep, and am known of Mine. As the Father knoweth Me, even so know I the Father; and I lay down My life for the sheep. And other sheep I have which are not of this fold; them also I must bring, and they shall hear My voice; and there shall be one fold, and one shepherd.

The Twentieth Sunday after Trinity

The holy Gospel is taken from the eleventh chapter of the Gospel according to St. Matthew, beginning at the twenty-eighth verse.

COME unto Me, all ye that labour and are heavy laden, and I will give you rest. Take My yoke upon you, and learn of Me, for I am meek and lowly in heart; and ye shall find rest unto your souls. For My yoke is easy and My burden is light. That it might be fulfilled which was spoken of Esaias the prophet, saying: Behold My servant, whom I have chosen; My beloved, in whom My soul is well pleased; I will put My Spirit upon Him, and He shall show judgement to the Gentiles. He shall not strive nor cry, neither shall any man hear His voice in the street. A bruised reed shall He not break, and smoking flax shall He not quench, till He send forth judgement unto victory; and in His Name shall the Gentiles trust.

The Twenty-First Sunday after Trinity

The holy Gospel is taken from the tenth chapter of the Gospel according to St. Matthew, beginning at the first verse.

WHEN Jesus had called unto Him His twelve disciples, He gave them power over unclean spirits, to cast them out, and to heal all manner of sickness and all manner of disease. And He said unto them: Behold, I send you forth as sheep in the midst of wolves; be ye therefore wise as serpents, and harmless as doves. The disciple is not above his Master, nor the servant above his lord. He that receiveth you receiveth Me, and he that receiveth Me receiveth Him that sent Me. Whosoever shall give to drink unto one of these little ones a cup of cold water only, in the name of a disciple, Amen I say unto you, he shall by no means lose his reward. He that loveth father or mother more than Me is not worthy of Me; and he that loveth son or daughter more than Me is not worthy of Me. And he that taketh not his cross and followeth after Me is not worthy of Me. He that findeth his life shall lose it; and he that loseth his life for My sake shall find it. But he that endureth to the end shall be saved.

The Twenty-Second Sunday after Trinity

The holy Gospel is taken from the sixth chapter of the Gospel according to St. Luke, beginning at the twenty-seventh verse.

I SAY unto you who hear: Love your enemies, do good to them who hate you, bless them that curse you, and pray for them who despitefully use you. And as ye would that men should do to you, do ye also to them likewise. Love ye your enemies, and do good and lend, hoping for nothing again; and your reward shall be great, and ye shall be the children of the Highest, for He is kind unto the unthankful and to the evil. Be ye therefore merciful, as your Father is merciful. Judge not, and ye shall not be judged; condemn not, and ye shall not be condemned; forgive, and ye shall be forgiven. Give, and it shall be given unto you; good measure, pressed down and shaken together, and running over, shall men give into your bosom. For with the same measure that ye mete withal it shall be measured to you again.

The Twenty-Third Sunday after Trinity

The holy Gospel is taken from the sixth chapter of the Gospel according to St. John, beginning at the twenty-eighth verse.

THEN said they unto Jesus: What shall we do, that we might work the works of God? Jesus answered and said unto them: This is the work of God, that ye believe on Him whom He hath sent. For the Bread of God is He who cometh down from heaven, and giveth life unto the world. Then said they unto Him: Lord, evermore give us this bread. And Jesus said unto them: I am the Bread of Life; he that cometh to Me shall never hunger; and he that believeth on Me shall never thirst. All that the Father giveth Me shall come to Me; and him that cometh to Me I will in no wise cast out. For this is the Father's will who hath sent Me, that of all which He hath given Me I should lose nothing, but should raise it up again at the last day. It is the spirit that quickeneth; the flesh profiteth nothing; the words that I speak unto you, they are spirit and they are life.

The Twenty-Fourth Sunday after Trinity

The holy Gospel is taken from the seventh chapter of the Gospel according to St. John, beginning at the sixteenth verse.

JESUS said: My doctrine is not Mine, but His that sent Me. If any man will do His will, he shall know of the doctrine whether it be of God. Judge not according to the appearance, but judge righteous judgement. If any man thirst, let him come unto Me and drink. I am the light of the world; he that followeth Me shall not walk in darkness, but shall have the light of life. If ye continue in My word, then are ye My disciples indeed; and ye shall know the truth, and the truth shall make you free.

The Sunday next before Advent

The holy Gospel is taken from the eighth chapter of the Gospel according to St. Luke, beginning at the fourth verse.

WHEN much people were gathered together Jesus spake unto them by a parable: A sower went out to sow his seed; and as he sowed some fell by the wayside, and it was trodden down, and the fowls of the air devoured it. And some fell upon a rock; and as soon as it was sprung up, it withered away, because it lacked moisture. And some fell among thorns; and the thorns sprang up with it, and choked it. And other fell on good ground, and sprang up, and bare fruit an hundredfold. He that hath ears to hear, let him hear. And His disciples asked Him: What might this parable be? And He said: Unto you it is given to know the mysteries of the kingdom of God; but to others in parables; that seeing they might not see, and hearing they might not understand. The parable is this: The seed is the word of God. Those by the wayside are they that hear; then cometh the adversary, and taketh away the word out of their hearts, lest they should understand and be saved. They on the rock are they who, when they hear, receive the word with joy; but these have no root, who for a while believe, and in time of temptation fall away. And that which fell among thorns are they, who, when they have heard, go forth, and are choked with cares and riches and pleasures of this life, and bring no fruit to perfection. But that on the good ground are they who in an honest and good heart, having heard the word, keep it, and bring forth fruit with patience.

If there be more than twenty-five Sundays after Trinity, the service(s) of some of those Sundays that were omitted after the Epiphany shall be used to supply as many as are wanting. And if there be fewer than twenty-five Sundays, those that remain over should be omitted, provided that this last gospel shall always be used upon the Sunday next before Advent.

The Baptism of Our Lord

The holy Gospel is taken from the third chapter of the Gospel according to St. Matthew, beginning at the first verse.

IN those days came John the Baptist, preaching in the wilderness of Judæa, and saying: Repent ye, for the kingdom of heaven is at hand. I indeed baptize you with water unto repentance; but He that cometh after me is mightier than I, whose shoes I am not worthy to bear; He shall baptize you with the Holy Ghost and with Fire. Then cometh Jesus from Galilee to Jordan unto John, to be baptized of Him. But John would have hindered Him, saying: I have need to be baptized of Thee, and comest Thou to me? And Jesus said unto him: Suffer it to be so now; for thus it becometh us to fulfil all righteousness. Then he suffered Him. And Jesus, when He was baptized, went up straightway out of the water; and, lo, the heavens were opened unto Him, and He saw the Spirit of God descending like a dove, and lighting upon Him. And, lo, a voice from heaven, saying: This is My beloved Son, in whom I am well pleased.

The Presentation of Our Lord in the Temple, or Candlemas

The holy Gospel is taken from the second chapter of the Gospel according to St. Luke, beginning at the twenty-second verse.

AND when the days of her purification according to the law of Moses were accomplished, they brought Him to Jerusalem to present Him to the Lord. And behold, there was a man in Jerusalem whose name was Simeon; and the same man was just and devout, waiting for the consolation of Israel; and the Holy Ghost was upon him. And it was revealed unto him by the Holy Ghost that he should not see death before he had seen the Lord's Christ And he came by the Spirit into the Temple; and when the parents brought in the child Jesus, to do for Him after the custom of the law, then took he Him up in his arms, and blessed God, and said: Lord, now lettest Thou Thy servant depart in peace, according to Thy word; for mine eyes have seen Thy salvation, which Thou hast prepared before the face of all people, to be a light to lighten the Gentiles, and to be the glory of Thy people Israel. And Joseph and His mother marvelled at those things which were spoken of Him.

The Annunciation of Our Lady

The holy Gospel is taken from the first chapter of the Gospel according to St. Luke, beginning at the twenty-sixth verse.

AND in the sixth month the Angel Gabriel was sent from God unto a city of Galilee named Nazareth, to a Virgin espoused to a man whose name was Joseph, of the house of David; and the Virgin's name was Mary. And the Angel came in unto her, and said: Hail, thou that art highly favoured, the Lord is with thee; blessed art thou among women. And when she saw him she was troubled at his saying, and cast in her mind what manner of salutation this should be. And the Angel said unto her: Fear not, Mary; for thou hast found favour with God. And behold, thou shalt bring forth a Son, and shalt call His name Jesus. He shall be great, and shall be called the Son of the Highest; and the Lord God shall give unto Him the throne of His father David. And He shall reign over the house of Jacob for ever; and of His kingdom there shall be no end. The Holy Ghost shall come upon thee, and the power of the Highest shall overshadow thee; therefore also that which is to be born of thee shall be called holy, the Son of God. And Mary said: Behold the handmaid of the Lord; be it unto me according to thy word.

St. Alban's Day

The holy Gospel is taken from the sixteenth chapter of the Gospel according to St. Matthew, beginning at the twenty-fourth verse.

THEN said Jesus unto His disciples: If any man will come after Me, let him deny himself, and take up his cross, and follow Me. For whosoever will save his life shall lose it; and whosoever will lose his life for My sake shall find it. For what is a man profited, if he shall gain the whole world, and lose his own soul? Or what shall a man give in exchange for his soul? For the Son of Man shall come in the glory of His Father with His Angels; and then He shall reward every man according to his works.

St. John Baptist's Day

The holy Gospel is taken from the first chapter of the Gospel according to St. Luke, beginning at the sixty-eighth verse.

BLESSED be the Lord God of Israel, for He hath visited and redeemed His people, and hath raised up a mighty salvation for us in the house of His servant David, as He spake by the mouth of His holy prophets, which have been since the world began; that we should be saved from our enemies, and from the hands of all that hate us; to show mercy towards our fathers, and to remember His holy covenant; that we, being delivered out of the hands of our enemies, might serve Him without fear, in holiness and righteousness before Him, all the days of our life. And thou, child, shalt be called the prophet of the Highest, for thou shalt go before the face of the Lord to prepare His ways; to give knowledge of salvation unto His people in the remission of their sins, through the tender mercy of our God, whereby the day-spring from on high hath visited us, to give light to them that sit in darkness and in the shadow of death, and to guide our feet into the way of peace.

St. Peter and the Holy Apostles

The holy Gospel is taken from the sixteenth chapter of the Gospel according to St. Matthew, beginning at the thirteenth verse.

WHEN Jesus came into the coasts of Cæsarea Philippi, He asked His disciples, saying: Who do men say that I, the Son of Man, am? And they said: Some say that Thou art John the Baptist, some Elias, and others Jeremias, or one of the prophets. He saith unto them: But who say ye that I am? And Simon Peter answered and said: Thou art the Christ, the Son of the Living God. And Jesus answered and said unto him: Blessed art thou, Simon Barjona; for flesh and blood hath not revealed it unto thee, but My Father who is in heaven. And I say also unto thee, that thou art Peter, and upon this rock I will build My Church; and the gates of hell shall not prevail against it. And I will give unto thee the keys of the kingdom of heaven, and whatsoever thou shalt bind on earth shall be bound in heaven; and whatsoever thou shalt loose on earth shall be loosed in heaven.

The Transfiguration

The holy Gospel is taken from the seventeenth chapter of the Gospel according to St. Matthew, beginning at the first verse.

JESUS taketh Peter, James, and John his brother, and bringeth them up into a high mountain apart, and was transfigured before them; and His face did shine as the sun, and His raiment was white as the light. And behold, there appeared unto them Moses and Elias talking with Him. Then said Peter unto Jesus: Lord, it is good for us to be here; if Thou wilt, let us make here three tabernacles; one for Thee, and one for Moses, and one for Elias. While he yet spoke, behold, a bright cloud overshadowed them; and behold, a voice out of the cloud, which said: This is My beloved Son, in whom I am well pleased; hear ye Him. And when the disciples heard it, they fell on their faces, and were sore afraid. But Jesus came and touched them, and said: Arise, and be not afraid. And when they had lifted up their eyes, they saw no man save Jesus only.

The Assumption of Our Lady

The holy Gospel is taken from the first chapter of the Gospel according to St. Luke, beginning at the twenty-sixth verse.

AND in the sixth month the Angel Gabriel was sent from God unto a city of Galilee named Nazareth, to a Virgin espoused to a man whose name was Joseph, of the house of David; and the Virgin's name was Mary. And the Angel came in unto her, and said: Hail, thou that art highly favoured, the Lord is with thee; blessed art thou among women. And when she saw him she was troubled at his saying, and cast in her mind what manner of salutation this should be. And the Angel said unto her: Fear not, Mary; for thou hast found favour With God. And behold, thou shalt bring forth a Son, and shalt call His name Jesus. He shall be great, and shall be called the Son of the Highest; and the Lord God shalt give unto Him the throne of His father David. And He shall reign over the house of Jacob for ever; and of His kingdom there shalt be no end. The Holy Ghost shall come upon thee, and the power of the Highest shall overshadow thee; therefore also that which is to be born of thee shalt be called holy, the Son of God. And Mary said: Behold the handmaid of the Lord; be it unto me according to thy word.

The same Gospel shall serve for seven days after.

The Nativity of Our Lady

The holy Gospel is taken from the first chapter of the Gospel according to St. Luke, beginning at the thirty-ninth verse.

MARY arose in those days, and went into the hill country, into a city of Juda, and entered into the house of Zacharias, and saluted Elizabeth. And it came to pass that when Elizabeth heard the salutation of Mary, she was filled with the Holy Ghost, and she spake out with a loud voice, and said: Blessed art thou among women, and blessed is the fruit of thy womb. Whence is this to me, that the mother of my Lord should come to me? For lo! as soon as the voice of thy salutation sounded in mine ears, the babe leaped in my womb for joy. Blessed is she that believeth; for there shall be a performance of those things which were told her from the Lord. And Mary said: My soul doth magnify the Lord, and my spirit hath rejoiced in God my Saviour. For He hath regarded the lowliness of His handmaiden; for behold from henceforth all generations shall call me blessed. For He that is mighty hath magnified me; and holy is His Name.

St. Michael and all Angels

The holy Gospel is taken from the eighteenth chapter of the Gospel according to St. Matthew, beginning at the first verse.

THEN came the disciples unto Jesus, saying: Who is the greatest in the Kingdom of heaven? And Jesus called a little child unto Him, and set him in the midst of them, and said: Amen, I say unto you, except ye be converted, and become as little children, ye shall not enter into the kingdom of heaven. Whosoever therefore shall humble himself as this little child, the same is greatest in the kingdom of heaven. And whoso shall receive one such little child in My Name receiveth Me. But whoso shall offend one of these little ones which believe in Me, it were better for him that a millstone were hanged about his neck, and that he were drowned in the depth of the sea. Woe unto the world because of offences; for it must needs be that offences come, but woe to that man by whom the offence cometh. Take heed that ye despise not one of these little ones; for I say unto you, that in heaven their Angels do always behold the face of My Father who is in heaven.

The same Gospel shall serve for seven days after.

All Saints' Day

The holy Gospel is taken from the twenty-fifth chapter of the Gospel according to St. Matthew, beginning at the thirty-fourth verse.

THEN shall the King say unto them on His right hand: Come, ye blessed of My Father, inherit the kingdom prepared for you from the foundation of the world. For I was an hungred, and ye gave Me meat; I was thirsty, and ye gave Me drink, I was a stranger and ye took Me in, naked and ye clothed Me, I was sick and ye visited Me, I was in prison and ye came unto Me. Then shall the righteous answer Him saying: Lord, when saw we Thee an hungred, and fed Thee, or thirsty and gave Thee drink? When saw we Thee a stranger and took Thee in, or naked and clothed Thee? Or when saw we Thee sick, or in prison, and came unto Thee? And the King shall answer and say unto them: Amen, I say unto you, inasmuch as ye have done it unto one of the least of these My brethren, ye have done it unto Me.

The same Gospel shall serve for seven days after, except on the Holy Day of All Souls.

All Souls' Day

The holy Gospel is taken from the fifth chapter of the Gospel according to St. John, beginning at the twenty-fourth verse.

AMEN, Amen, I say unto you, he that heareth My word, and believeth on Him that sent Me, hath everlasting life, and shall not come into condemnation; but is passed from death unto life. Amen, Amen, I say unto you, the hour is coming, and now is, when the dead shall hear the voice of the Son of God; and they that hear shall live. For as the Father hath life in Himself, so hath He given to the Son to have life in Himself, and hath given Him authority to execute judgement also, because He is the Son of Man. Marvel not at this; they that have done good shall come unto the resurrection of life; and they that have done evil unto the resurrection of judgement.

The Patron Saint of a Country

The holy Gospel is taken from the sixteenth chapter of the Gospel according to St. Matthew, beginning at the twenty-fourth verse.

THEN said Jesus unto His disciples: If any man will come after Me, let him deny himself, and take up his cross, and follow Me. For whosoever will save his life shall lose it; and whosoever will lose his life for My sake shall find It. For what is a man profited, if he shall gain the whole world, and lose his own soul? Or what shall a man give in exchange for his soul? For the Son of Man shall come in the glory of His Father with His Angels; and then He shall reward every man according to his works.

The Patron Saint of a Church

The Gospel shall be the same as appointed for the Patron Saint of a Country.

Days of National Rejoicing

The Holy Gospel is taken from the first chapter of the Gospel according to St. Luke, beginning at the sixty-eighth verse.

BLESSED be the Lord God of Israel, for He hath visited and redeemed His people, and hath raised up a mighty salvation for us in the house of His servant David, as He spake by the mouth of His holy prophets, which have been since the world began: that we should be saved from our enemies and from the hands of all that hate us, to perform the mercy promised to our forefathers, and to remember His holy covenant; that He would grant unto us that we, being delivered out of the hands of our enemies, might serve Him without fear in holiness and righteousness before Him, all the days of our life. And thou, child, shalt be called the prophet of the Highest, for thou shalt go before the face of the Lord to prepare His ways; to give knowledge of salvation unto His people in the remission of their sins, through the tender mercy of our God, whereby the day-spring from on high hath visited us, to give light to them that sit in darkness and in the shadow of death, and to guide our feet into the way of peace.

Days of National Thanksgiving
(ESPECIALLY FOR PEACE)

The holy Gospel is taken from the twelfth chapter of the Gospel according to St. John, beginning at the twenty-third verse.

JESUS said: The hour is come that the Son of Man should be glorified. Amen, Amen, I say unto you: Except a corn of wheat fall into the ground and die, it abideth alone; but if it die, it bringeth forth much fruit. He that loveth his life shall lose it; and he that hateth his life in this world shall keep it unto life eternal. If any man serve Me, let him follow Me: and where I am, there shall also My servant be. And I, if I be lifted up from the earth, will draw all men unto Me.

At a Harvest Festival

The holy Gospel is taken from the twelfth chapter of the Gospel according to St. Luke, beginning at the sixth verse.

And he spake a parable unto them, saying, The ground of a certain rich man brought forth plentifully: And he thought within himself, saying, What shall I do, because I have no room where to bestow my fruits? And he said, This will I do: I will pull down my barns, and build greater; and there will I bestow all my fruits and my goods. But God said unto him, Thou fool, this night thy soul shall be required of thee: then whose shall those things be, which thou hast provided? So is he that layeth up treasure for himself, and is not rich toward God. And he said unto his disciples, Therefore I say unto you, Take no thought for your life, what ye shall eat; neither for the body, what ye shall put on. The life is more than meat, and the body is more than raiment. [So] seek not ye what ye shall eat, or what ye shall drink, neither be ye of doubtful mind. For all these things do the nations of the world seek after: and your Father knoweth that ye have need of these things.

Common of Saints

The holy Gospel is taken from the fifth chapter of the Gospel according to St. Matthew, beginning at the second verse.

JESUS taught His disciples, saying: Blessed are the poor in spirit; for theirs is the kingdom of heaven. Blessed are they that mourn; for they shall be comforted. Blessed are the meek; for they shall inherit the earth. Blessed are they which do hunger and thirst after righteousness; for they shall be filled. Blessed are the merciful; for they shall obtain mercy. Blessed are the pure in heart; for they shall see God. Blessed are the peacemakers; for they shall be called the children of God. Blessed are they which are persecuted for righteousness' sake; for theirs is the kingdom of heaven. Blessed are ye, when men shall revile you, and persecute you, and shall say all manner of evil against you falsely, for My sake. Rejoice, and be exceeding glad; for great is your reward in heaven; for so persecuted they the prophets which were before you.

The Nuptial Eucharist

The holy Gospel is taken from the fifteenth chapter of the Gospel according to St. John, beginning at the first verse.

I am the true vine, and My Father is the husbandman. Every branch in Me that beareth not fruit He taketh away: and every branch that beareth fruit, He purgeth it, that it may bring forth more fruit. Now ye are clean through the word which I have spoken unto you. Abide in Me, and I in you. As the branch cannot bear fruit of itself, except it abide in the vine; no more can ye, except ye abide in Me. I am the vine, ye are the branches; he that abideth in Me, and I in him, the same bringeth forth much fruit: for without Me ye can do nothing. If a man abide not in Me, he is cast forth as a branch, and is withered; and men gather them, and cast them into the fire, and they are burned. If ye abide in Me, and My words abide in you, ye shall ask what ye will, and it shall be done unto you. Herein is My Father glorified, that ye bear much fruit; so shall ye be My disciples. As the Father hath loved Me, so have I loved you; continue ye in My love. If ye keep My commandments, ye shall abide in My love; even as I have kept My Father's commandments, and abide in His love. These things have I spoken unto you, that My joy might remain in you, and that your joy might be full.

The Requiem Eucharist

The holy Gospel is taken from the eleventh chapter of the Gospel according to St. John, beginning at the twenty-first verse.

Then said Martha unto Jesus: Lord, if Thou hadst been here, my brother had not died. But I know that even now, whatsoever Thou wilt ask of God, God will give it Thee. Jesus saith unto her: Thy brother shall rise again. Martha saith unto Him: I know that he shall rise again in the resurrection at the last day. Jesus said unto her: I am the Resurrection and the Life; he that believeth in Me, though he were dead, yet shall he live. And whosoever liveth and believeth in Me shall never die. Believest thou this? She saith unto Him: Yea, Lord; I believe that thou art the Christ, the Son of God, who should come into world.

In the case of children, the following Gospel is used:

The holy Gospel is taken from the tenth chapter of the according to St. Mark, beginning at the thirteenth verse.

And they brought young children to Him, that He should touch them; and His disciples rebuked those that brought them. But when Jesus saw it, He was much displeased, and said unto them: Suffer the little children to come unto Me, and forbid them not; for of such is the kingdom of God. Amen, I say unto you: Whosoever shall not receive the kingdom of God as a little child, he shall not enter therein. And He took them up in His arms, put His hands upon them, and blessed them.

Ordination of Deacons

One of the newly-ordained Deacons, vested in dalmatic, reads the Gospel.

The holy Gospel is taken from the fifteenth chapter of the Gospel according to St. Luke, beginning at the third verse.

AND HE spake this parable unto them, saying: What man of you, having an hundred sheep, if he lose one of them, doth not leave the ninety and nine in the wilderness, and go after that which is lost, until he find it? And when he hath found it, he layeth it on his shoulders, rejoicing. And when he cometh home, he calleth together his friends and neighbours, saying unto them: Rejoice with me, for I have found my sheep which was lost. I say unto you, that likewise joy shall be in heaven over one sinner that repenteth, more than over ninety and nine just persons, who need no repentance.

Ordination of Priests

One of the newly-ordained Priests, vested in chasuble, reads the Gospel

The holy Gospel is taken from the twentieth chapter of the Gospel according to St. John, beginning at the nineteenth verse, and from the twenty-eighth chapter of the Gospel according to St. Matthew, beginning at the eighteenth verse.

THE SAME day at evening, being the first day of the week, when the doors were shut where the disciples were assembled for fear of the Jews; came Jesus, and stood in the midst, and saith unto them: Peace be unto you. Then were the disciples glad, when they saw the Lord. Then said Jesus unto them again: Peace be unto you; as my Father hath sent me, even so send I you. And when He had said this, He breathed on them, and saith unto them: Receive ye the Holy Ghost. Whosesoever sins ye remit, they are remitted unto them; and whosesoever sins ye retain, they are retained.

Jesus spake unto them, saying: All power is given unto me in heaven and in earth. Go ye therefore and teach all nations, baptizing them in the Name of the Father, and of the Son, and of the Holy Ghost, teaching them to observe all things whatsoever I have commanded you; and lo, I am with you alway, even unto the consummation of the age.

Consecration of a Bishop

The holy Gospel is taken from the fourteenth chapter of the Gospel according to St. John, beginning at the fifteenth verse.

JESUS said unto His disciples: I will pray the Father, and He shall give you another Comforter, that He may abide with you for ever; even the Spirit of Truth, whom the world cannot receive, because it seeth Him not, neither knoweth Him; but ye know Him; for He dwelleth with you, and shall be in you. I will not leave you comfortless; I will come to you. Yet a little while, and the world seeth Me no more; but ye see Me; because I live, ye shall live also. The Comforter, who is the Holy Ghost, whom the Father will send in My Name, He shall teach you all things, and bring all things to your remembrance, whatsoever I have said unto you. Peace I leave with you, My peace I give unto you; not as the world giveth, give I unto you. Let not your heart be troubled, neither let it be afraid.

Consecration of a Church
or its
Dedication Festival

The holy Gospel is taken from the fourteenth chapter of the Gospel according to St. John, beginning at the sixth verse.

JESUS said: I am the Way, the Truth and the Life; no man cometh unto the Father but by Me. He that hath seen Me hath seen the Father; for I am in the Father, and the Father in Me. I and My Father are one; as the Father hath loved Me, so have I loved you; and this is My commandment, that ye love one another, as I have loved you. When the Comforter is come, whom I will send unto you from the Father, even the Spirit of Truth, who proceedeth from the Father, He shall testify of Me. And ye also shall bear witness, because ye have been with Me from the beginning. By this shall all men know that ye are My disciples, if ye have love one to another.

On the Anniversary of the Consecration of a Bishop
or
Special Celebration for a Bishop or Synod

The holy Gospel is taken from the fourteenth chapter of the Gospel according to St. John, beginning at the sixteenth verse.

JESUS said unto His disciples: I will pray the Father, and He shall give you another Comforter, that He may abide with you for ever; even the Spirit of Truth, whom the world cannot receive, because it seeth Him not, neither knoweth Him; but ye know Him; for He dwelleth with you, and shall be in you. I will not leave you comfortless; I will come to you. Yet a little while, and the world seeth Me no more; but ye see Me; because I live, ye shall live also. The Comforter, who is the Holy Ghost, whom the Father will send in My Name, He shall teach you all things, and bring all things to your remembrance, whatsoever I have said unto you. Peace I leave with you, My peace I give unto you: not as the world giveth, give I unto you. Let not your heart be troubled, neither let it be afraid.

Special Celebration for Unity among Christians

The holy Gospel is taken from the fifteenth chapter of the Gospel according to St. John, beginning at the first verse.

I AM the true vine, and My Father is the Husbandman. I am the Vine, ye are the branches. Abide in Me, and I in you. As the branch cannot bear fruit of itself, except it abide in the vine; no more can ye, except ye abide in Me. He that abideth in Me, and I in him, the same bringeth forth much fruit; for without Me ye can do nothing. Herein is My Father glorified, that ye bear much fruit; so shall ye be My disciples. As the Father hath loved Me, so have I loved you; continue ye in My love. If ye keep My commandments, ye shall abide in My love; even as I have kept My Father's commandments, and abide in His love. These things have I spoken unto you, that My joy might remain in you, and that your joy might be full. These things I command you, that ye love one another.

𝕾pecial Celebration for the 𝕾ick

The holy Gospel is taken from the seventh chapter of the Gospel according to St. Luke, beginning at the second verse.

NOW a certain centurion's servant, who was very dear unto him, was sick and ready to die. And when he heard of Jesus, he sent unto Him the elders of the Jews, beseeching Him that He would come and heal his servant. And when they came to Jesus, they besought Him instantly, saying that he was worthy for whom He should do this: for he loveth our nation, and he hath built us a synagogue. Then Jesus went with them. And when He was now not far from the house, the centurion sent friends to Him, saying unto Him: Lord, trouble not Thyself; for I am not worthy that Thou shouldest enter under my roof (wherefore neither thought I myself worthy to come unto Thee); but say in a Word, and my servant shall be healed. For I also am a man set under authority, having under me soldiers, and I say unto one: Go, and he goeth; and to another, Come, and he cometh; and to my servant, Do this, and he doeth it. When Jesus heard these things, He marvelled at him, and turned Him about, and said unto the people that followed Him: I say unto you, I have not found so great faith; no, not in Israel. And they that were sent, returning to the house, found the servant whole that had been sick.

The Gospel on page 40 may also be used.

Deacon. **Cleanse my heart and my lips, O God, who by the hand of Thy Seraph didst cleanse the lips of the prophet Isaiah with a burning coal from Thine altar, and in Thy loving-kindness so purify me that I may worthily proclaim Thy holy Gospel; through Christ our Lord. ℟ Amen.**

The Celebrant blesses the Gospeller in the following words:

May the Lord be in thy ✠ heart and on thy ✠ lips, that through thy heart the love of God may shine forth, and through thy lips His power be made manifest. ℟. Amen.

www.ingramcontent.com/pod-product-compliance
Lightning Source LLC
Chambersburg PA
CBHW030758150426
42813CB00068B/3214/J